Born in 1943

by

Kerry Butters.

__Born in 1943__

Millennium: 2nd millennium

Centuries: 19th century – **20th century** – 21st century

Decades: 1910s 1920s 1930s – **1940s** – 1950s 1960s 1970s

Years: 1940 1941 1942 – **1943** – 1944 1945 1946

1943 (MCMXLIII) was a common year starting on Friday (dominical letter C) of the Gregorian calendar, the 1943rd year of the Common Era (CE) and *Anno Domini* (AD) designations, the 943rd year of the 2nd millennium, the 43rd year of the 20th century, and the 4th year of the 1940s decade.

Contents

Events

January

- January 1 – WWII: The Soviet Union announces that 22 German divisions have been encircled at Stalingrad, with 175,000 killed and 137,650 captured.
- January 4
  - WWII: Greek-Polish athlete and saboteur Jerzy Iwanow-Szajnowicz is executed by the Germans at Kaisariani.
  - Culbert Olson, 29th Governor of California, is succeeded by Earl Warren.
- January 11 – The United States and United Kingdom give up territorial rights in China.
- January 13 – 36 people are executed and 200 arrested in anti-Nazi protests in Sofia.
- January 14–24 – WWII: Casablanca Conference: Franklin D. Roosevelt, President of the United States; Winston Churchill, Prime Minister of the United Kingdom; and Generals

Charles de Gaulle and Henri Giraud of the Free French forces meet secretly at the Anfa Hotel in Casablanca, Morocco, to plan the Allied European strategy for the next stage of the war.

- January 15
    - WWII: Guadalcanal Campaign – Operation Ke: Japanese forces begin to withdraw from Guadalcanal in the Solomon Islands.
    - The world's largest office building, The Pentagon, is dedicated in Arlington, Virginia.
- January 16 – Iraq declares war on the Axis powers.
- January 18
    - WWII: Soviet officials announce that the Red Army has broken the Wehrmacht's siege of Leningrad as part of Operation Iskra, opening a narrow land corridor to the city. Georgy Zhukov is promoted to Marshal of the Soviet Union.
    - The first Warsaw Ghetto Uprising begins.
- January 22
    - WWII: Battle of Buna–Gona ends with American and Australian forces securing control of the territory of Papua.
    - The Holocaust: Over 4,000 Jews are detained in Nazi-occupied Marseille as part of "Action Tiger" before being transported to extermination camps in Poland.
- January 23
    - WWII: British forces capture Tripoli from the Italians.
    - Duke Ellington plays at New York City's Carnegie Hall for the first time.
    - American critic and commentator Alexander Woollcott suffers an eventually fatal heart attack during a regular

broadcast of the CBS Radio round-table program *People's Platform*.

- January 27 – WWII: 50 bombers mount the first all American air raid against Germany: Wilhelmshaven is the target.
- January 29
  - Nazi German police arrest alleged necrophiliac and serial killer Bruno Lüdke.
  - United States Marine Corps Women's Reserve (MCWR) created.
- January 29–30 – WWII: Battle of Rennell Island – The Imperial Japanese Navy resists the United States Navy's attempt to interrupt the withdrawal of Japanese forces from Guadalcanal in the last major naval battle of the Guadalcanal Campaign.
- January 29–31 – WWII: Battle of Wau – Australian forces with United States support resist a Japanese advance in the New Guinea campaign.

February

- February 2 – WWII: In Russia, the Battle of Stalingrad comes to an end with the surrender of the German 6th Army.
- February 3 – WWII: The Four Chaplains of the U.S. Army are among those drowned when their ship, *Dorchester*, is struck by a German torpedo in the North Atlantic.
- February 5 – Lt. General Frank M. Andrews is selected to command the U.S. armies in Europe, while General Dwight D. Eisenhower is assigned command in North Africa; General Andrews will serve only three months before dying in an airplane crash.
-

- February 7 – WWII:
    - North Atlantic convoy SC 118 is attacked by U-boats sinking eight ships.
    - In the United States, it is announced that shoe rationing will go into effect in 2 days.
- February 9 – WWII:
    - Guadalcanal Campaign in the Solomon Islands ends with United States forces in command of Guadalcanal, the evacuation of Japanese forces in Operation Ke having been completed two days earlier.
    - Massacres of Poles in Volhynia and Eastern Galicia by the Ukrainian Insurgent Army begin with the Parośla I massacre within the Reichskommissariat Ukraine.
- February 10–March 3 – Mohandas Gandhi (under arrest by forces of the British Raj in Pune as a member of the Quit India Movement) keeps a hunger strike to protest at his imprisonment.
- February 14 – WWII: Rostov-on-Don in Russia is liberated.
- February 14–17 – WWII: Battle of Sidi Bou Zid: In the Tunisia Campaign, German Panzer divisions commanded by Hans-Jürgen von Arnim are victorious over the United States Army.
- February 16 – WWII: The Soviet Union reconquers Kharkov, but is later driven out in the Third Battle of Kharkov.
- February 18
    - In a *Sportpalast* speech in Berlin, German Propaganda Minister Joseph Goebbels declares a "total war" against the Allies, tacitly admitting that Nazi Germany faces serious dangers.
    - The Nazis arrest the members of the White Rose German Resistance movement.

- February 19–25 – WWII: Battle of Kasserine Pass: German General Erwin Rommel's Afrika Korps and other Axis forces launch an offensive against Allied defenses in Tunisia; it is the United States' first major battle defeat of the war. On February 22 an Anglo-American force halts the German advance near Thala, forcing the Germans to retreat, US bombers harass the retreating Panzers.
- February 20
    - American movie studio executives agree to allow the Office of War Information to censor movies.
    - The Parícutin volcano begins to appear in a cornfield in Mexico.
- February 21 – WWII: North Atlantic convoy ON 166 is attacked by U-boats sinking eleven ships.
- February 22 – Members of White Rose are executed in Nazi Germany.
- February 23–24 – Cavan Orphanage Fire: 35 girls and a cook from St Joseph's Orphanage, an industrial school at Cavan, Ireland, are killed in a fire in their dormitories. A subsequent inquiry absolves the Poor Clares of blame.
- February 27 – Smith Mine disaster: an explosion at Smith Mine #3 in Bearcreek, Montana, United States kills 74 coal miners.
- February 28 – Operation Gunnerside: 6 Norwegians led by Joachim Rønneberg successfully attack the heavy water plant at Vemork.

March

A low level attack on a Japanese ship during the Battle of the Bismarck Sea

Jewish prisoners being deported from the Kraków Ghetto

- March – Publication in New York of exiled French aviator Antoine de Saint-Exupéry's self-illustrated children's novella *The Little Prince*, the all-time best-selling book originated in French.
- March–December – History of computing hardware: Construction of British prototype Mark I Colossus computer, the world's first totally *electronic* programmable computing device, to assist in cryptanalysis of German signals at Bletchley Park.
- March 1 – Heinz Guderian becomes the Inspector-General of the Armoured Troops for the German Army.

- March 1 –2 – WWII: Koriukivka massacre – Mass murder of the inhabitants of Koriukivka in the Ukraine by German SS troops.
- March 2 – WWII: Battle of the Bismarck Sea – United States and Australian forces sink Japanese convoy ships.
- March 3 – 173 people are killed in a crush while trying to enter an air-raid shelter at Bethnal Green, London.
- March 4 – The 15th Academy Awards ceremony is held in Los Angeles. *Mrs. Miniver* wins the Best Picture award.
- March 5 – The Gloster Meteor, the first operational military jet aircraft for the Allies, has its first test flight, in England.
- March 6 – WWII: North Atlantic convoy SC 121 is attacked by U-boats sinking seven ships.
- March 9 – Şükrü Saracoğlu forms the new government of Turkey (14th government; Şükrü Saracoğlu had served twice as a prime minister).
- March 10 – Banco Bradesco is founded in Marília, São Paulo, Brazil.
- March 13 – The Holocaust: Nazi German forces liquidate the Jews of the Kraków Ghetto in Occupied Poland.
- March 14 – WWII: British submarine HMS *Thunderbolt* is sunk off Sicily by an Italian corvette, the second time this vessel has been lost with all hands.
- March 15 – WWII:
    - The Italian submarine *Leonardo da Vinci* sinks the Canadian Pacific liner RMS *Empress of Canada* off Sierra Leone. Nearly half of the 392 fatalities are Italian prisoners of war.
    - German forces recapture Kharkov after four days of house-to-house fighting against Soviet troops, ending the month-long Third Battle of Kharkov.

- March 16–19 – WWII: 22 ships from Convoys HX 229/SC 122 and one U-boat are sunk in the largest North Atlantic U-boat "wolfpack" attack of the war.
- March 17 (Saint Patrick's Day) – Éamon de Valera, Taoiseach of the Republic of Ireland, makes the speech "The Ireland That We Dreamed Of", commonly called the "comely maidens" speech, in Dublin Castle.
- March 22 – WWII: Khatyn massacre – The entire population of Khatyn in Belarus is burnt alive by the German occupation forces.
- March 23 – The drugs Vicodin and Lortab are first produced in Germany.
- March 26 – WWII: Battle of the Komandorski Islands: In the Aleutian Islands, the battle begins when United States Navy forces intercept Japanese troops attempting to reinforce a garrison at Kiska.
- March 27 – WWII: British Royal Navy escort carrier HMS *Dasher* (D37) is destroyed by an accidental explosion in the Firth of Clyde, killing 379 of the crew of 528.
- March 28 – In Italy a ship full of weapons and ammunition explodes in the port of Naples, killing 600.
- March 31 – Rodgers and Hammerstein's *Oklahoma!* opens on Broadway, heralds a new era in "integrated" stage musicals, becomes an instantaneous stage classic, and goes on to be Broadway's longest-running musical up to that time (1948).

April

- April 3 – Shipwrecked steward Poon Lim is rescued by Brazilian fishermen after being adrift for 130 days.

- April 13 – WWII: Radio Berlin announces the discovery by Wehrmacht of mass graves of Poles killed by Soviets in the Katyn massacre.
- April 19 – Albert Hofmann self-administers the psychedelic drug LSD (which he first synthesized in 1938) for the first time in history, and records the details of his experience.
- April 19 – The Holocaust: The Warsaw Ghetto Uprising begins when Nazi troops enter the Warsaw Ghetto to round up remaining Jews.
- April 21 – WWII: Worst bombing of Aberdeen, Scotland, killing 125 people.
- April 25 – Easter occurs on the latest possible date (last time 1886; next time 2038) in the Western Christian Church.
- April 26 – The Easter Riots in Uppsala, Sweden.
- April 27 – The U.S. Federal Writers' Project ceases operation.

May

This photograph, from the Stroop Report, shows captured fighters in the Warsaw Ghetto Uprising.

The Möhne Dam breached following Operation Chastise, carried out by the "Dambusters" of the RAF.

- May 6 – WWII: Six U-boats are sunk after sinking 12 ships from Convoy ONS 5 in the last major North Atlantic U-boat "wolfpack" attack of the war.
- May 9–12 – Japanese troops carry out the Changjiao massacre in Changjiao, Hunan, China.
- May 11 – WWII: American troops invade Attu in the Aleutian Islands, in an attempt to expel occupying Japanese forces.
- May 12 – The Trident Conference begins in Washington, D.C., with Franklin D. Roosevelt and Winston Churchill taking part.
- May 13 – WWII: German Afrika Korps and Italian troops in North Africa surrender to Allied forces.
- May 14
    - The Australian Hospital Ship *Centaur* is sunk off the coast of Queensland by Japanese submarine *I-177*, killing 268 of the 332 medical personnel and civilian crew aboard.

- 358th Bombardment Squadron, 303d Bombardment Group B-17F *Hell's Angels* is the first USAAF bomber to complete 25 missions.
- May 15 – The Comintern is dissolved in Moscow.
- May 16–17 – WWII: Operation Chastise (the 'Dambuster Raid') takes place: No. 617 Squadron RAF use bouncing bombs to breach German dams in the Ruhr Valley.
- May 16 – Holocaust: The Warsaw Ghetto Uprising ends.
- May 17 – WWII:
  - The United States Army contracts with the University of Pennsylvania's Moore School to develop the computer ENIAC.
  - The *Memphis Belle's* crew becomes the first aircrew in the 8th Air Force to complete its 25-mission tour of duty. The aircraft and crew are the first to return to the U.S. intact for a War Bond drive.
- May 19 – Winston Churchill addresses a joint session of the United States Congress.
- May 29 – Norman Rockwell's illustration of *Rosie the Riveter* first appears on the cover of *The Saturday Evening Post*.
- May 30 – The Holocaust: Dr. Josef Mengele begins his service as a medical officer in the Auschwitz-Birkenau concentration camp.

June

- June 1 – BOAC Flight 777, a DC-3 with registration G-AGBB (formerly KLM PH-ALI, *Ibis*), on a scheduled passenger flight, is shot down over the Bay of Biscay by eight German Junkers Ju 88s; all 17 persons aboard perish, including the actor Leslie Howard. There is speculation that the downing was an attempt to kill the Prime Minister of the United Kingdom, Winston Churchill, as the Germans may have had wrong information he was aboard.

- June 3 – The Zoot Suit Riots erupt between military personnel and Mexican American youths in East Los Angeles.
- June 4 – A military coup d'état in Argentina ousts Ramón Castillo.
- June 8 – WWII: Japanese battleship *Mutsu* is destroyed by an accidental magazine explosion in Hashirajima anchorage
- June 20 – Race riots in Detroit: killed 34 people — 25 African Americans, nine whites — wounded hundreds more and damaged and destroyed property worth millions.
- June 21 – WWII: British saboteurs blow up the strategically significant railway viaduct at Asopos in Greece.
- June 22 – WWII: The U.S. Army 45th Infantry Division lands in North Africa, prior to training at Arzew, French Morocco.
- June 30 – United States Civilian Conservation Corps abolished.
- June (late) – The Holocaust: The last trainload of Jewish prisoners is moved from Bełżec extermination camp in Occupied Poland (for gassing at Sobibór) and for the remainder of the year the Nazis make efforts to obliterate the site.

July

The U.S. Liberty ship SS *Robert Rowan* explodes during the Allied invasion of Sicily, July 11, 1943.

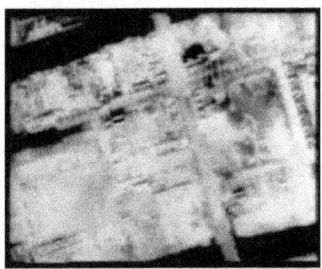

The bombing of Hamburg during 1943.

- July 1 – United States Women's Army Corps (WAC) converted to full status.
- July 4 – 1943 Gibraltar B-24 crash: The aircraft carrying General Władysław Sikorski, Prime Minister of the Polish government-in-exile, crashes, killing him and fifteen others, leading to a lasting controversy over the circumstances.
- July 5 – WWII:
  - Battle of Kursk – The largest tank battle in history begins.
  - A fleet sets sail for the Allied invasion of Sicily.
  - Conclusion of the National Bands Agreement in Greece.

- July 6 – WWII: Americans and Japanese fight the Battle of Kula Gulf off Kolombangara.
- July 10 (0245 GMT (4:45 am local time)) – WWII: Allied invasion of Sicily: The Allied invasion of Axis-controlled Europe begins with landings on the island of Sicily off mainland Italy by the Seventh United States Army and the British Eighth Army including the 1st Canadian Infantry Division.
- July 11 – WWII:
  - United States Army forces make an assault on Piano Lupo, just outside Gela, Sicily.
  - Massacres of Poles in Volhynia and Eastern Galicia by the Ukrainian Insurgent Army within the Reichskommissariat Ukraine (Volhynia) peak.
- July 12 – WWII: Main engagement of the Battle of Prokhorovka – The Wehrmacht and the Red Army fight to a draw in one of the largest tank battles in military history.
- July 19 – WWII: Rome is bombed by the Allies for the first time in the war.
- July 24 – WWII: Operation Gomorrha begins: British and Canadian aeroplanes bomb Hamburg by night; the American planes bomb the city by day. By the end of the operation in November, 9,000 tons of explosives will have killed more than 42,000 people and destroyed 280,000 buildings.

Mussolini

- July 25 – Benito Mussolini, the Fascist Prime Minister of Italy since 1925, is arrested after the Grand Council of Fascism withdraws its support. "Il Duce" is replaced by General Pietro Badoglio.

August

B-24d's fly over Ploieşti during Operation Tidal Wave.

Mackenzie King, Franklin D. Roosevelt and Winston Churchill at the 1943 Quebec Conference.

- August 1 – Operation Tidal Wave: 177 B-24 Liberator bombers from the U.S. Army Air Force bomb oil refineries at Ploiești, Romania.
- August 2 – WWII: John F. Kennedy's Motor Torpedo Boat *PT-109* is rammed by a destroyer.
- August 4 – WWII: The aircraft carrier USS *Intrepid* (CV-11) is launched at Newport News, Virginia.
- August 5 – WWII:
    - United States Women Airforce Service Pilots (WASPs) formed, consolidating the Women's Auxiliary Ferrying Squadron (WAFS) and Women Airforce Service Pilots (WFTD).
    - John F. Kennedy and crew are found by Solomon Islands coastwatchers Biuku Gasa and Eroni Kumana with their dugout canoe.
- August 6 – WWII: Battle of Vella Gulf: Americans defeat a Japanese convoy off Kolombangara, as the U.S. Army drives the Japanese out of Munda airfield on New Georgia.
- August 14 – WWII: Rome is declared an open city by the Italian government, with Italy offering to demilitarize the

capital in return for an Allied agreement not to bomb the city further.

- August 14 – The Quadrant Conference begins in Quebec City; Canadian Prime Minister MacKenzie King meets with Winston Churchill and Franklin D. Roosevelt.
- August 17 – WWII:
  - The US 7th Army under General George S. Patton meets the British 8th Army under General Montgomery in Messina, Sicily, completing the Allied invasion of Sicily.
  - Operation Hydra: The British Royal Air Force sets out to bomb the Peenemünde Army Research Center to disrupt the German V-weapons programme.
- August 23 – WWII: The Battle of Kursk ends with a serious strategic defeat for the German forces.
- August 24 – WWII: – Heinrich Himmler is named Reichminister of the Interior in Germany .
- August 26 – WWII: Lord Mountbatten named Supreme Allied Commander for Southeast Asia.
- August 28 – WWII: King Boris III of Bulgaria dies under suspicious circumstances; his 6-year-old son, Simeon II (who would be elected in 2001 as Prime Minister under the name Simeon Sakskoburggotski), ascends to the throne.
- August 29 – WWII: Occupation of Denmark – Germany dissolves the Danish government after it refuses to deal with a wave of strikes and disturbances to the satisfaction of the German authorities.

- September 3 – WWII: Allied invasion of Italy: Mainland Italy is invaded by Allied forces under General Sir Bernard Montgomery, for the first time in the war.
- September 5 – WWII: The 503rd Parachute Regiment under American General Douglas MacArthur lands and occupies Nadzab, just east of the port city of Lae in northeastern Papua New Guinea.
- September 7 – Gulf Hotel fire: A fire at the Gulf Hotel in Houston, Texas kills 55.
- September 8 –
  - WWII: United States General Dwight D. Eisenhower publicly announces the surrender of Italy to the Allies.
  - WWII: Frascati air raid: The USAAF bombs the German General Headquarters for the Mediterranean zone.
  - The first classes commence at Grace University in Omaha, Nebraska.
- September 9 – Bertolt Brecht's play *Life of Galileo* (German: *Leben des Galilei*) receives its first theatrical production at the Schauspielhaus Zürich.
- September 12 – WWII: Gran Sasso raid – German paratroopers rescue Mussolini from imprisonment, in *Unternehmen Eiche* ("Operation Oak").
- September 16 – WWII: The Salerno Mutiny occurs when soldiers of the British Army's X Corps refuse postings to new units.
- September 17 – WWII: Villefranche-de-Rouergue Mutiny – a group of pro-Partisan soldiers led by Ferid Džanić and others within the 13th Waffen Mountain Division of the SS

Handschar (1st Croatian) training in Occupied France rise against Nazi German troops in the Division; the revolt is rapidly suppressed.

- September 22–October 2 – WWII: Landing at Scarlet Beach on the Huon Peninsula of New Guinea by Allied forces, the first time Australian troops have made an opposed amphibious landing since the Gallipoli Campaign of 1915.
- September 23 – WWII: The Italian Social Republic ("Republic of Salò") is founded in northern Italy as a puppet state of Nazi Germany.
- September 27 – WWII: Four days of Naples begins: a popular uprising drives German occupying forces from the city.

October

- October 1 – WWII: United States forces enter liberated Naples.
- October 6 – WWII: Americans and Japanese fight the naval Battle of Vella Lavella.
- October 7 – WWII: The Naples Naples post-office bombing kills 100.
- October 10 – The Order of Bogdan Khmelnitsky is instituted in the Soviet Union.
- October 13 – WWII: The new government of Italy sides with the Allies and declares war on Germany.
- October 14
  - WWII: During the Second Raid on Schweinfurt, the United States VIII Bomber Command suffers so many losses that it loses air supremacy over Germany for several months.

- The Holocaust: Uprising in Sobibór extermination camp; about half the inmates escape. Three days later, the camp is closed.
- José P. Laurel takes the oath of office as President of the Philippines (Second Philippine Republic).
- October 17 – WWII: The last commerce raider *hilfskreuzer Michel*, is sunk off Japan by United States submarine *Tarpon*.
- October 18 – Chiang Kai-shek takes the oath of office as Chairman of the National Government of China.
- October 19 – WWII: Allied aircraft sink the German-controlled cargo ship MS *Sinfra* in the Mediterranean, killing over 2,000 people, mostly Italian military internees.
- October 21 – Lucie Aubrac and others in her French Resistance cell liberate Raymond Aubrac from Gestapo imprisonment.
- October 22 – WWII: The British Royal Air Force delivers a highly destructive airstrike on the German industrial and population center of Kassel.
- October 24 – WWII: British Royal Navy destroyer HMS *Eclipse* (H08) is sunk by a mine in the Aegean Sea with the loss of 119 of the ship's company and 134 troops.
- October 28 – Alleged date of the Philadelphia Experiment, in which the destroyer escort USS *Eldridge* (DE-173) was supposed to be rendered invisible to human observers for a brief period.
- October 30
  - WWII: Signing of Moscow Declarations: the Declaration of the Four Nations on general security, by the United States, United Kingdom, Soviet Union and Republic of China; and the Declarations on Italy, Austria and Atrocities by the first three governments.

- The Merrie Melodies animated cartoon *Falling Hare*, one of the only shorts with Bugs Bunny getting out-smarted, is released in the United States.

November

Chiang Kai-shek, Franklin D. Roosevelt and Winston Churchill at the Cairo Conference, 25 November 1943.

The first Lebanese flag hand drawn and signed by the deputies of the Lebanese parliament, November 11, 1943. The French Mandate ends and Lebanon gains independence in November 1943.

Joseph Stalin, Franklin D. Roosevelt, and Winston Churchill on the verandah of the Soviet Embassy in Tehran during the Tehran Conference

- November 1 – WWII: Operation Goodtime: United States Marines land on Bougainville Island in the Solomon Islands.
- November 2 – WWII:
    - In the early morning hours, American and Japanese ships fight the inconclusive Battle of Empress Augusta Bay off Bougainville Island.
    - WWII: British troops in Italy reach the Garigliano River.
- November 5 WWII: First Bombing of the Vatican: Four bombs are dropped on the neutral Vatican City; the aircraft responsible is never certainly identified.
- November 9 – Agreement for foundation of the United Nations Relief and Rehabilitation Administration signed by 44 countries in the White House, Washington, D.C.
- November 10 – Execution of the Lübeck martyrs, four men of religion, for supposedly treasonable views.
- November 14 – Leonard Bernstein, substituting at the last minute for ailing principal conductor Bruno Walter, directs the New York Philharmonic in its regular Sunday afternoon broadcast concert over CBS Radio. The event receives front-page coverage in *The New York Times* the following day.

- November 15 – Porajmos: German SS leader Heinrich Himmler orders that Gypsies and "part-Gypsies" be put "on the same level as Jews and placed in Nazi concentration camps."
- November 16
    - WWII: After flying from Britain, 160 American bombers strike a hydro-electric power facility and heavy water factory in German-controlled Vemork, Norway.
    - WWII: A Japanese submarine sinks the surfaced U.S. submarine USS *Corvina* near Chuuk Lagoon (Truk).
- November 18 – WWII: Battle of Berlin – The British Royal Air Force opens its bombing campaign against Berlin with 440 planes causing only light damage and killing 131. The RAF loses 9 aircraft and 53 aviators.
- November 19 – The Holocaust: Inmates of Janowska concentration camp near Lwów (at this time in German-occupied Poland), stage a failed uprising, after which the SS liquidates the camp, resulting in at least 6,000 deaths.
- November 20 – WWII: Battle of Tarawa: United States Marines land on Tarawa and Makin atolls in the Gilbert Islands (Kiribati from 1979) and take heavy fire from Japanese shore guns.
- November 22 –26 – WWII: Cairo Conference ("Sextant") – President of the United States Franklin D. Roosevelt, Prime Minister of the United Kingdom Winston Churchill and Chairman of the National Government of China Chiang Kai-shek meet at Cairo in Egypt to discuss ways to defeat Japan in the Pacific War.
- November 22 – Lebanon gains independence on ending of the French Mandate.

- November 23 – The Deutsches Opernhaus on Bismarckstraße in the Berlin district of Charlottenburg is destroyed in an air raid (It is reopened in 1961 as the Deutsche Oper Berlin).
- November 25 – WWII: Americans and Japanese fight the naval Battle of Cape St. George between Buka and New Ireland.
- November 28 – WWII: Tehran Conference: U.S. President Franklin D. Roosevelt, British Prime Minister Winston Churchill and Soviet leader Joseph Stalin meet in Tehran to discuss war strategy. On November 30, they establish an agreement concerning a planned June 1944 invasion of Europe codenamed Operation Overlord.
- November 29 – The second session of AVNOJ, the Anti-Fascist Council of National Liberation of Yugoslavia, is held in Jajce, Bosnia and Herzegovina, to determine the post-war ordering of the country.

December

- December 2 – WWII: Bari chemical warfare disaster: A surprise Luftwaffe air raid on Bari in Italy sinks 28 Allied ships in the harbor, including the American Liberty ship SS *John Harvey*, releasing its secret cargo of mustard gas bombs, inflating the number of casualties.
- December 3
  - In reprisal for an act of sabotage, the SS and Gestapo execute 100 Warsaw Tramway workers.
  - Edward R. Murrow delivers his classic "Orchestrated Hell" broadcast over CBS Radio, describing a Royal Air Force nighttime bombing raid on Berlin.

- December 4
  - WWII: In Yugoslavia, resistance leader Marshal Tito proclaims a provisional democratic Yugoslav government-in-exile.
  - The Great Depression officially ends in the United States: With unemployment figures falling fast due to WWII-related employment, U.S. President Franklin D. Roosevelt closes the Works Progress Administration.
- December 4 – WWII: Bolivia declares war on Romania and Hungary.
- December 7 – Chiara Lubich starts the humanitarian Focolare Movement in Trento, Italy.
- December 13 – WWII: Massacre of Kalavryta: The occupying 117th Jäger Division (Wehrmacht) machine-gun all adult males from Kalavryta in Greece, subsequently burning the town.
- December 15 – WWII: American and Australian forces began the Battle of Arawe as a diversion before a larger landing at Cape Gloucester on New Britain in Papua New Guinea.
- December 20 – A military coup is staged in Bolivia.
- December 24 – WWII: U.S. General Dwight D. Eisenhower becomes Supreme Allied Commander Europe. He establishes Supreme Headquarters Allied Expeditionary Force in London.
- December 30 – Subhas Chandra Bose sets up a pro-Japanese Indian government at Port Blair, India.

Date unknown

- Bengal Famine.
- History of the cooperative movement: Father José María Arizmendiarrieta sets up a polytechnic school at Mondragón

in the Spanish Basque Country (predecessor of the University of Mondragón) which inspires creation of the Mondragon Corporation.

- Arana Hall, a residential college of the University of Otago in Dunedin, New Zealand, is founded.
- Jacques-Yves Cousteau co-invents, with Émile Gagnan, the first commercially successful open circuit type of scuba diving equipment, the Aqua-lung.
- Publication of Martin Noth's groundbreaking work of Old Testament scholarship *Überlieferungsgeschichtliche Studien: Die sammelnden und bearbeitenden Geschichtswerke im Alten Testament.*

Births

January

Janis Joplin

Princess Margriet of the Netherlands

- January 1
  - Stanley Kamel, American actor (d. 2008)
  - Don Novello (aka "Father Guido Sarducci"), American comedian
- January 2 – Barış Manço, Turkish singer and television personality (d. 1999)
- January 4 – Doris Kearns Goodwin, American writer
- January 6 – Terry Venables, English football manager
- January 7 – Sadako Sasaki, Japanese atomic bomb sickness victim (d. 1955)
- January 9 – Freddie Starr, English comedian and singer
- January 10 – Jim Croce, American singer-songwriter (d. 1973)
- January 11 – Jim Hightower, American radio host and author
- January 13 – Richard Moll, American television actor
- January 14
  - Ralph M. Steinman, Canadian immunologist and cell biologist; Nobel laureate (d. 2011)
  - Holland Taylor, American stage, film and television actress
  - José Luis Rodríguez, Venezuelan singer
- January 15 – Dame Margaret Beckett, British politician
- January 18 – Kay Granger, American politician
- January 19
  - Janis Joplin, American rock singer (d. 1970)
  - Princess Margriet of the Netherlands
  - Haruo Yasuda
- January 20 – Mel Hague, English singer and author

- January 22
  - Tamás Cseh, Hungarian composer, singer and actor (d. 2009)
  - Marília Pêra, Brazilian actress (d. 2015)
- January 24
  - Janice Raymond, American second-wave feminist activist
  - Sharon Tate, American actress and model murdered by the "Manson Family" (d. 1969)
- January 25
  - Dagmar Berghoff, German radio and television presenter
  - Roy Black, German singer (d. 1991)
  - Tobe Hooper, American film director
- January 26 – César Gutiérrez, Venezuelan Major League Baseball player (d. 2005)
- January 28 – John Beck, American actor
- January 29
  - Tony Blackburn, British radio disc jockey
  - Rudy Regalado, Venezuelan musician (d. 2010)

February

Blythe Danner

Joe Pesci

Horst Köhler

George Harrison

- February 2 – Erkan Geniş, Turkish artist
- February 3 – Blythe Danner, American actress
- February 4 – Alberto João Jardim, Portuguese politician
- February 5
  - Nolan Bushnell, American video game pioneer
  - Michael Mann, American film director, writer, and producer
  - Craig Morton, American football player

- February 8 – Creed Bratton, American actor and musician
- February 9
  - Joe Pesci, American actor
  - Joseph E. Stiglitz, American economist, Nobel Prize laureate
- February 12 – Wacław Kisielewski, Polish pianist (d. 1986)
- February 14 – Maceo Parker, American musician (James Brown, P-Funk)
- February 15 – Elke Heidenreich, German author, TV presenter and journalist
- February 18 – Graeme Garden, Scottish writer, comedian, and actor
- February 19
  - Homer Hickam, American author and retired NASA engineer
  - Tim Hunt, British biochemist, recipient of the Nobel Prize in Physiology or Medicine
- February 20
  - Moshe Cotel, American composer and pianist (d. 2008)
  - Antonio Inoki, Japanese professional wrestler
  - Mike Leigh, British film director
- February 21 – David Geffen, American record executive and film producer
- February 22 – Horst Köhler, German former president
- February 23 – Fred Biletnikoff, American football player and coach
- February 24 – Hristo Prodanov, Bulgarian mountaineer
- February 25 – George Harrison, British musician (The Beatles) (d. 2001)
- February 26 – Bill Duke, American actor and director
- February 27 – Morten Lauridsen, American composer

- February 28 – Donnie Iris, American rock singer and guitarist (The Jaggerz, Wild Cherry, Donnie Iris and the Cruisers)

March

Lynn Redgrave

David Cronenberg

Ratko Mladić

George Benson

Eric Idle

John Major

Christopher Walken

- March 1
  - Gil Amelio, American entrepreneur
  - Richard H. Price, American physicist
- March 2
  - Zygfryd Blaut, Polish footballer (d. 2005)
  - Tony Meehan, British drummer (The Shadows) (d. 2005)
  - Peter Straub, American author
- March 3 – Trond Mohn, Norwegian billionaire
- March 4
  - Lucio Dalla, Italian singer and songwriter (d. 2012)
  - Zoltán Jeney, Hungarian composer
- March 5 – Lucio Battisti, Italian singer and songwriter (d. 1998)
- March 8 – Lynn Redgrave, English actress (d. 2010)
- March 9
  - Bobby Fischer, American chess player (d. 2008)
  - Charles Gibson, American television journalist
- March 13 – André Téchiné, French film director
- March 15
  - David Cronenberg, Canadian film director
  - Sly Stone, American singer
- March 16
  - Helen Armstrong, American violinist (d. 2006)
  - Kim Mu-saeng, South Korean actor (d. 2005)
- March 18 – Kevin Dobson, American actor
- March 19
  - Mario J. Molina, Mexican chemist, Nobel Prize laureate
  - Mario Monti, Prime Minister of Italy (2011 – 2013), Italian Senator
  -

- March 20
  - Douglas Tompkins, American conservationist and businessman (d. 2015)
  - Gerard Malanga, American poet and photographer
- March 21
  - István Gyulai, Hungarian sports official (d. 2006)
  - Vivian Stanshall, English comedian, writer, artist, broadcaster, and musician (d. 1995)
- March 22
  - George Benson, American guitarist and singer-songwriter.
  - Bruno Ganz, Swiss actor
  - Keith Relf, British rock musician (The Yardbirds) (d. 1976)
- March 25 – Paul Michael Glaser, American actor
- March 26 – Bob Woodward, American journalist
- March 29
  - Eric Idle, English actor, writer, and composer
  - John Major, Prime Minister of the United Kingdom (1990 – 1997)
  - Vangelis, Greek musician and composer
- March 31
  - Motiur Rahman Nizami, Bangladeshi politician and convicted war criminal (d. 2016)
  - Christopher Walken, American actor
-

April

John Eliot Gardiner

- April 2 – Caterina Bueno, Italian singer (d. 2007)
- April 5 – Max Gail, American actor
- April 8 – Miller Farr, American football player
- April 10
  - Andrzej Badeński, Polish athlete (d. 2008)
  - Margaret Pemberton, English writer
- April 11 – Harley Race, American professional wrestler
- April 16 – Petro Tyschtschenko, German businessman
- April 19 – Claus Theo Gärtner, German actor
- April 20 – John Eliot Gardiner, English conductor
- April 22 – Louise Glück, American poet and 12th US Poet Laureate
- April 23
  - Dominik Duka, Czech Roman Catholic bishop and theologian
  - Fighting Harada, Japanese boxer
  - Frans Koppelaar, Dutch painter
  - Hervé Villechaize, French-born actor (d. 1993)
- April 24 – Richard Sterban, American singer (The Oak Ridge Boys)
- April 25
  - Alan Feduccia, American paleornithologist

- James G. Mitchell, Canadian computer scientist
- April 28 – John O. Creighton, American astronaut
- April 30 – Frederick Chiluba, former President of Zambia (d. 2011)

May

Michael Palin

Ólafur Ragnar Grímsson

- May 1 – Vassal Gadoengin, Nauruan politician (d. 2004)
- May 5 – Michael Palin, English comedian and television presenter
- May 6 – Grange Calveley, British writer and artist
- May 10 – Richard (Dick) Darman, American federal government official and businessman
- May 13 – Kurt Trampedach, Danish artist
- May 14
    - Jack Bruce, British musician and songwriter (d. 2014)

- ○ Ólafur Ragnar Grímsson, President of Iceland
- May 17 – Tuanku Syed Sirajuddin, King of Malaysia
- May 22 – Betty Williams, Northern Irish political activist, co-recipient of the Nobel Peace Prize
- May 25 – Jessi Colter, American singer and composer
- May 26 – Erica Terpstra, Dutch swimmer, politician and president of the Dutch Olympic Committee
- May 27
  - ○ Bruce Weitz, American actor
  - ○ Cilla Black, English singer and entertainer (d. 2015)
- May 30 – James Chaney, American civil rights worker (d. 1964)
- May 31
  - ○ Sharon Gless, American actress
  - ○ Joe Namath, American football player

June

Malcolm McDowell

Klaus von Klitzing

- June 1
  - Lorrie Wilmot, South African cricketer (d. 2004)
  - Kuki Gallmann, Kenyan writer and poet
- June 2 – Ilayaraaja, Indian composer
- June 3 – John Burgess, Australian game show host and actor
- June 4 – Joyce Meyer, Christian author and speaker
- June 6 – Richard Smalley, American chemist, Nobel Prize laureate (d. 2005)
- June 7
  - Chan Hung-lit, Hong Kong actor (d. 2009)
  - Nikki Giovanni, American poet
- June 8 – Colin Baker, British actor
- June 13 – Malcolm McDowell, British actor
- June 14 – Jim Sensenbrenner, American politician
- June 15
  - Johnny Hallyday, French singer and actor
  - Poul Nyrup Rasmussen, Prime Minister of Denmark
- June 16 – Joan Van Ark, American actress
- June 17
  - Newt Gingrich, American politician
  - Barry Manilow, American pop musician
- June 18 – Barry Evans, English actor (d. 1997)
- June 21 – Marika Green French-Swedish actress
- June 22 – Klaus Maria Brandauer, Austrian actor
- June 23 – Patrick Bokanowski, French filmmaker
  - James Levine, American conductor
  - Vint Cerf, American internet pioneer
- June 26 – John Beasley, American actor
- June 27 – Rico Petrocelli, baseball player
- June 28
  - Jens Birkemose, Danish painter

- o Klaus von Klitzing, German physicist, Nobel Prize laureate
- June 29
  - o Maureen O'Brien, British actress
  - o Soon-Tek Oh, Korean-American actor
- June 30 – Ahmed Sofa, Bangladeshi writer (d. 2001)

July

Mick Jagger

- July 1 – Jeff Wayne, American musician
- July 3
  - o Judith Durham, Australian singer
  - o Kurtwood Smith, American actor
- July 4
  - o Konrad "Conny" Bauer, German trombonist
  - o Geraldo Rivera, American reporter and talk show host
- July 5 – Curt Blefary, American baseball player (d. 2001)
- July 7 – Joel Siegel, American film critic (d. 2007)
- July 8 – Guido Marzulli, Italian painter
- July 9 – Soledad Miranda, Spanish actress (d. 1970)
- July 10 – Arthur Ashe, American tennis player (d. 1993)
- July 12
  - o Christine McVie, British rock keyboardist and singer (Fleetwood Mac)

- o Walter Murch, American film editor and sound designer
- July 15 – Jocelyn Bell Burnell, British astrophysicist
- July 16
  - o Reinaldo Arenas, Cuban writer (d. 1990)
  - o Jimmy Johnson, American football coach and television analyst
- July 19
  - o David Griffin, British actor
  - o Han Sai Por, Singaporean sculptor
- July 20
  - o Christopher Murney, American actor and vocal artist
  - o Wendy Richard, British actress (d. 2009)
- July 21
  - o Edward Herrmann, American actor (d. 2014)
  - o Bob Shrum, political consultant
- July 23
  - o Dr. Randall Forsberg, American nuclear freeze advocate (d. 2007)
  - o Bob Hilton, American game show announcer and host
  - o Larry Manetti, American actor
- July 25 – Erika Steinbach, German politician
- July 26 – Mick Jagger, English rock singer
- July 28 – Richard Wright, British musician (Pink Floyd) (d. 2008)

August

Pervez Musharraf

Robert De Niro

Pino Presti

- August 2 – Max Wright, American actor
- August 3 – Clarence Wijewardena, Sri Lankan musician (d. 1996)
- August 4 – Barbara Saß-Viehweger, German politician, lawyer and civil law notary
- August 4 – Bjørn Wirkola, Norwegian ski jumper
- August 5 – Nelson Briles, American baseball player (d. 2005)

- August 6 – Jim Hardin, former Baltimore Orioles, New York Yankees and Atlanta Braves pitcher (d. 1991)
- August 9 – Ken Norton, American boxer and actor (d. 2013)
- August 11
  - Abigail Folger, American heiress and murder victim (d. 1969)
  - Pervez Musharraf, Pakistani general and leader
- August 13 – Roberto Micheletti, President of Honduras
- August 17
  - Robert De Niro, American actor
  - Yukio Kasaya, Japanese ski jumper
- August 18 – Gianni Rivera, Italian footballer
- August 20 – Sylvester McCoy, British actor
- August 23
  - Bobby Diamond, American actor
  - Pino Presti, Italian bassist, arranger, composer, conductor, record producer
- August 27 – Tuesday Weld, American actress
- August 28
  - Surayud Chulanont, Thailand's 24th Prime Minister
  - Lou Piniella, American baseball player and manager
  - Jihad Al-Atrash, Lebanese actor and voice actor
- August 29 – Arthur B. McDonald, Canadian astrophysicist, Nobel Prize laureate
- August 30
  - Tal Brody, American-born Israeli basketball player
  - R. Crumb, American artist and illustrator
  - Altovise Davis, American entertainer (d. 2009)
  - Jean-Claude Killy, French skier
- August 31 – Leonid Ivashov, Russian general

September

Lech Wałęsa

Mohammad Khatami

- September 1 – Don Stroud, American actor and surfer
- September 3 – Valerie Perrine, American actress and model
- September 5 – Dulce Saguisag, Filipino politician and former DSWD Secretary (d. 2007)
- September 6
  - Richard J. Roberts, English biochemist and molecular biologist, recipient of the Nobel Prize in Physiology or Medicine
  - Roger Waters, English musician (Pink Floyd)
- September 7 – Lena Valaitis, Lithuanian-German Schlager singer
- September 9 – Art LaFleur, American actor
- September 10
  - Daniel Truhitte, American actor

- Neale Donald Walsch, American author of the popular books Conversations with God
- September 11
  - Gilbert Proesch, Italian-born artist (Gilbert and George)
  - Raymond Villeneuve, Canadian terrorist
- September 13 – Mildred D. Taylor, American writer
- September 14 – Irwin Goodman, Finnish singer (d. 1991)
- September 16 – Oskar Lafontaine, German politician
- September 19 – Joe Morgan, American Hall of Fame baseball player
- September 22 – Toni Basil, American musician and video artist
- September 23 – Julio Iglesias, Spanish singer and songwriter
- September 28 – J. T. Walsh, American actor (d. 1998)
- September 29
  - Mohammad Khatami, 5th President of Iran
  - Lech Wałęsa, President of Poland, recipient of the Nobel Peace Prize
- September 30
  - Johann Deisenhofer, German biochemist, Nobel Prize laureate
  - Ian Ogilvy, English actor

October

Chevy Chase

Catherine Deneuve

- October 1 – Jean-Jacques Annaud, French film director
- October 2 – Franklin Rosemont, American poet (d. 2009)
- October 6 – Michael Durrell, American actor
- October 7 – Oliver North, American military officer, military historian, political commentator, author and television host
- October 8 – Chevy Chase, American comedian and actor
- October 11 – John Nettles, English actor and writer
- October 14 – Lois Hamilton, American model, actress and artist (d. 1999)
- October 15 – Penny Marshall, American actress, director and producer
- October 16 – Paul Rose, Canadian terrorist
- October 18
    - Birthe Rønn Hornbech, Danish politician
    - Christine Charbonneau, Canadian francophone singer and songwriter (d. 2014)
- October 20 – Noreen Corcoran, American child actress and director (d. 2016)
- October 22 – Catherine Deneuve, French actress
- October 27 – Carmen Argenziano, American actor
- October 28 – Cornelia Froboess, German actress
- October 29 – Don Simpson, American film producer, screenwriter, and actor (d. 1996)

- October 31 – Paul Frampton, English physicist

November

Joni Mitchell

Michael Spence

- November 1 – Jacques Attali, French economist
- November 3 – Bert Jansch, Scottish folk musician (d. 2011)
- November 4 – Chuck Scarborough, American news anchor
- November 5
    - Friedman Paul Erhardt, German-American pioneering television chef (d. 2007)
    - Sam Shepard, American playwright and actor
- November 7
    - Stephen Greenblatt, American literary critic
    - Joni Mitchell, Canadian musician
    - Michael Spence, American economist, Nobel Prize laureate
- November 11 – Doug Frost, Australian swimming coach

- November 12 – Wallace Shawn, American actor
- November 13
  - Roberto Boninsegna, Italian footballer
  - Jay Sigel, American golfer
- November 14
  - Peter Norton, American software engineer and businessman
  - Rafael Leonardo Callejas, President of Honduras
- November 17 – Lauren Hutton, American actress and model
- November 19 – Aurelio Monteagudo, Cuban Major League Baseball player (d. 1990)
- November 20
  - Mie Hama, Japanese actress
  - Marek Tomaszewski, Polish pianist
- November 21 – Larry Mahan, American rodeo cowboy
- November 22
  - Peter Adair, American filmmaker (d. 1996)
  - Yvan Cournoyer, Canadian ice hockey player
  - Billie Jean King, American tennis player
  - William Kotzwinkle, American novelist and screenwriter
- November 23 – Denis Sassou Nguesso, President of the Republic of the Congo
- November 24 – Dave Bing, American mayor and longtime NBA player
- November 26 – Marilynne Robinson, American writer
- November 28 – Randy Newman, American musician

December

Jim Morrison

John Kerry

Keith Richards

Sir Ben Kingsley

- December 2
  - Wayne Allard, U.S Senator from Colorado
  - William Wegman, American photographer
- December 5 – Eva Joly, Norwegian-born French magistrate
- December 8
  - José Carbajal, Uruguayan singer, composer and guitarist (d. 2010)
  - Larry Martin, American paleontologist (d. 2013)
  - Jim Morrison, American rock musician (d. 1971)
  - Bodo Tümmler, German Olympic middle-distance runner
- December 11 – John Kerry, American politician, diplomat
- December 12
  - Gianni Russo, American actor
  - Grover Washington, Jr., American saxophonist (d. 1999)
- December 13 – Ferguson Jenkins, Canadian baseball player
- December 15 – Lucien den Arend, Dutch sculptor
- December 17 – Ron Geesin, British musician and songwriter (Pink Floyd)
- December 18 – Keith Richards, English rock guitarist and songwriter
- December 19
  - Sam Kelly, English actor (d. 2014)
  - Ross M. Lence, American political scientist (d. 2006)
  - Jimmy Mackay, Australian football player (d. 1998)
- December 20 – Jacqueline Pearce, English actress
- December 21 – Jack Nance, American actor (d. 1996)
- December 23
  - Elizabeth Hartman, American actress (d. 1987)
  - Harry Shearer, American actor, comedian and screenwriter

- December 24
  - Tarja Halonen, President of Finland
  - James A. Johnson, American business leader and philanthropist
- December 25 – Hanna Schygulla, German actress
- December 28
  - Keith Floyd, British chef (d. 2009)
  - Craig MacIntosh, noted American comics illustrator
  - Richard Whiteley, English television presenter (d. 2005)
- December 31
  - John Denver, American singer-songwriter, actor, activist, and humanitarian (d. 1997)
  - Sir Ben Kingsley, British actor

Date unknown

- Kim Tai-chung, Korean martial artist and former actor and Bruce Lee double (d. 2011)
- Tang Da Wu, Singaporean artist
- James Goldstein, LA businessman and NBA basketball aficionado
- Alfredo Rostgaard, Cuban visual artist (d. 2004)

Deaths

January

Nikola Tesla

- January 3 – Bid McPhee, American baseball player and MLB Hall of Famer (b. 1859)
- January 4 – Jerzy Iwanow-Szajnowicz, Greek-Polish athlete and resistance member (b. 1911)
- January 5 – George Washington Carver, African-American botanist (b. 1864)
- January 7 – Nikola Tesla, Serbian-American electrical engineer and inventor (b. 1856)
- January 8 – Richard Hillary, Battle of Britain Spitfire pilot, author (*The Last Enemy*; b. 1919)
- January 11 – Agustín Pedro Justo, 23rd President of Argentina; b. 1876)
- January 12 – Jan Campert, Dutch journalist and writer (Neuengamme concentration camp; b. 1902)
- January 13 – Henner Henkel, German tennis champion (b. 1915)
- January 15 – Eric Knight, American author (b. 1897)
- January 20 – Baron Max Wladimir von Beck, former Ministers-President of Austria (b. 1854)
- January 21 – Robert Henry English, American admiral (b. 1888)
- January 23 – Alexander Woollcott, American critic (b. 1887)
- January 26 – Nikolai Vavilov, Russian and Soviet botanist and geneticist (b. 1887)
- January 29
    - Henriette Caillaux, murderer, French socialite and wife of former French prime minister (b. 1874)
    - Vladimir Kokovtsov, 4th Chairman of the Council of Ministers of the Russian Empire (b. 1853)

February

David Hilbert

- February 4 – Frank Calder, the first NHL President (b. 1877)
- February 5
    - Sim Gokkes, Dutch composer (in Auschwitz concentration camp) (b. 1897)
    - W. S. Van Dyke, American director (b. 1889)
- February 11 – Bess Houdini, American wife of Harry Houdini (b. 1876)
- February 14 – David Hilbert, German mathematician (b. 1862)
- February 20 -- Ernest Guglielminetti – Swiss physician (b. 1862)
- February 22
    - Tamara Drasin, Russian-born American signer and actress (b. ca. 1905)
    - Christoph Probst, German White Rose resistance member (executed) (b. 1919)
    - Ben Robertson, American novelist, journalist, and war correspondent (b. 1903)
    - Hans Scholl, German White Rose resistance member (executed) (b. 1918)

- ○ Sophie Scholl, German White Rose resistance member (executed) (b. 1921)
- February 26 – Theodor Eicke, German Nazi official (killed in action) (b. 1892)

March

Sergei Rachmaninoff

- March 6 – Jimmy Collins, American baseball player and MLB Hall of Famer (b. 1870)
- March 9 – Otto Freundlich, German painter and sculptor (b. 1878)
- March 10 – Tully Marshall, American actor (b. 1864)
- March 19 – Frank Nitti, Italian-American gangster (suicide) (b. 1886)
- March 20 – Heinrich Zimmer, German Indologist and historian (b. 1890)
- March 27 – George Monckton-Arundell, 8th Viscount Galway, English politician, 5th Governor-General of New Zealand (b. 1882)
- March 28
  - ○ Sergei Rachmaninoff, Russian composer (b. 1873)
  - ○ Robert W. Paul, English film director (b. 1869)
- March 31 – Pavel Milyukov, Russian politician, founder and leader of the Constitutional Democratic Party (b. 1859)

April

- April 3 – Conrad Veidt, German actor (b. 1893)
- April 7 – Alexandre Millerand, French president (b. 1859)
- April 8
  - Harry Baur, French actor (b. 1880)
  - Richard Sears, American tennis champion (b. 1861)
- April 9 – Philip Slier, Dutch Jewish typesetter (in Sobibór extermination camp) (b. 1923)
- April 13 – Oskar Schlemmer, German painter, sculptor, designer and choreographer (b. 1888)
- April 18 – Isoroku Yamamoto, Japanese admiral (b. 1884)
- April 24
  - Kenneth Whiting, United States Navy officer and submarine and naval aviation pioneer (b. 1881)
  - Kurt von Hammerstein-Equord, German general (b. 1878)
- April 30 – Beatrice Webb, English sociologist, economist, historian and social reformer (b. 1858)

May

- May 1 – Johan Oscar Smith, Norwegian Christian leader, founder of Brunstad Christian Church (b. 1871)
- May 3 – Frank Maxwell Andrews, American general (plane crash) (b. 1884)
- May 7 – Fethi Okyar, former prime minister of Turkey (b. 1880)
- May 17
  - Johanna Elberskirchen, German feminist (b. 1864)
  - Montagu Love, English actor (b. 1877)

- May 19 – Kristjan Raud, Estonian painter and drawer (b. 1865)
- May 20 – John Stone Stone, American physicist and inventor (b. 1869)
- May 22 – Helen Taft, wife of U.S. President William Howard Taft (b. 1861)
- May 26 – Edsel Ford, American buinessman, president of Ford Motor Company (b. 1893)
- May 29 – Yasuyo Yamasaki, Imperial Japanese Army officer (killed in action) (b. 1891)
- May 31 – Helmut Kapp, German Gestapo official

June

Karl Landsteiner

- June 1 – Leslie Howard, British actor (b. 1893)
- June 2 – Nile Kinnick, American athlete and Heisman Trophy winner (b. 1918)
- June 4 – Kermit Roosevelt, American explorer and author (b. 1889)
- June 11 – Heisuke Abe, Japanese general (b. 1886)
- June 26 – Karl Landsteiner, Austrian biologist and physician (b. 1868)

July

- July 4 – Władysław Sikorski, Polish politician (b. 1881)
- July 6 – Teruo Akiyama, Japanese admiral (killed in action) (b. 1891)
- July 8
    - Jean Moulin, French resistance fighter (b. 1899)
    - Sir Harry Oakes, American-born English gold mine owner (murdered) (b. 1874)
- July 12
    - Shunji Isaki, Japanese admiral (killed in action) (b. 1892)
    - Cecilia Loftus, stage actress (b. 1876)
- July 13 – Luz Long, German long jump athlete (b. 1913)
- July 21
    - Charley Paddock, American athlete (b. 1900)
    - Louis Vauxcelles, French art critic (b. 1870)

August

- August 9 – Chaim Soutine, Russian painter (born 1893)
- August 12 – Bobby Peel, English cricketer (b. 1857)
- August 14 – Joe Kelley, American baseball player and MLB Hall of Famer (b. 1871)
- August 18 – Hans Jeschonnek, German general (suicide) (b. 1899)
- August 21 – Henrik Pontoppidan, Danish writer, Nobel Prize laureate (b. 1857)
- August 24
    - Simone Weil, French philosopher (b. 1909)
    - Ettore Muti, Italian Fascist politician (murdered) (b. 1902)

- August 26 – Ted Ray, British golfer (b. 1877)
- August 28 – King Boris III of Bulgaria (b. 1894)

September

- September 1 – Charles Atangana, Cameroonian chief (b. ca. 1880)
- September 6 – Reginald McKenna, British Chancellor of the Exchequer 1915–1916 (b. 1863)
- September 7 – Karlrobert Kreiten, German pianist (executed) (b. 1916)
- September 8 – Julius Fučík, Czech resistance fighter (executed) (b. 1903)
- September 9 – Carlo Bergamini, Italian admiral (killed in action) (b. 1888)
- September 13 – Ugo Cavallero, General of the Italian Army (suicide) (b. 1880)
- September 19 – Germaine Cernay, French mezzo soprano (b. 1900)
- September 23 – Elinor Glyn, British writer (b. 1864)

October

Pieter Zeeman

- October 2 – Carlos Blanco Galindo, 38th President of Bolivia (b. 1882)

- October 5 – Leon Roppolo, American musician (b. 1902)
- October 9 – Pieter Zeeman, Dutch physicist, Nobel Prize laureate (b. 1865)
- October 12 – Max Wertheimer, Austro-Hungarian psychologist (b. 1880)
- October 14
  - Rudolf Beckmann, German SS officer (Sobibór uprising) (b. 1910)
  - Siegfried Graetschus, German SS officer (Sobibór uprising) (b. 1916)
  - Johann Niemann, German SS officer (Sobibór uprising) (b. 1913)
- October 19 – Camille Claudel, French sculptor (b. 1864)
- October 21 – Dudley Pound, British admiral (b. 1877)
- October 23 – Ben Bernie, American jazz pianist (b. 1891)
- October 30 – Max Reinhardt, Austrian director (b. 1873)

November

- November 5 – Idhomene Kosturi, 9th Prime Minister of Albania (b. 1873)
- November 7 – Dwight Frye, American actor (b. 1899)
- November 13 – Maurice Denis, French painter (b. 1870)
- November 22
  - Lorenz Hart, American lyricist (b. 1895)
  - Keiji Shibazaki, Japanese admiral (killed in action) (b. 1894)
- November 23 – Charles Ray, American actor (b. 1891)
- November 24
  - Doris "Dorie" Miller, American sailor, Pearl Harbor survivor (killed in action) (b. 1919)

- Henry M. Mullinnix, American admiral (killed in action) (b. 1892)
- November 26
  - Kiyoto Kagawa, Japanese admiral (killed in action) (b. 1895)
  - Edward "Butch" O'Hare, American fighter pilot (killed in action) (b. 1914)

December

John Harvey Kellogg

- December 1 – Damrong Rajanubhab, Thai prince and historian (b. 1862)
- December 9 – Georges Dufrénoy, French post-impressionnist painter (b. 1870)
- December 14 – John Harvey Kellogg, American doctor (b. 1852)
- December 15 – Fats Waller, African-American jazz pianist (b. 1904)
- December 20 – Edward L. Beach, Sr., American naval officer and author (b. 1867)
- December 22 – Beatrix Potter, British children's author and illustrator (b. 1866)
- December 25 – William Irving, German-born American film actor (b. 1893)

- December 26 – Erich Bey, German admiral (killed in action in Battle of the North Cape) (b. 1898)
- December 30 – Hobart Bosworth, American film actor, director, writer, and producer (b. 1867)
- December 27 – Rupert Julian, New Zealand-born film director (b. 1879)

Nobel Prizes

- Physics – Otto Stern
- Chemistry – George de Hevesy
- Physiology or Medicine – Carl Peter Henrik Dam, Edward Adelbert Doisy
- Literature – not awarded
- Peace – not awarded

In the News

The Pentagon, considered to be the world's largest office building is completed.

The Allied forces invade Italy during July of 1943.

German forces liquidate the Jewish ghetto in Krakow.

The Dambuster Raids by RAF 617 Sqdn on 17th May on German dams.

Popular Films - For Whom the Bell Tolls, Heaven Can Wait, Lassie Come Home, The Titanic 1943.

Car Tax Registration introduced in US.

Due to shortages in Copper the U.S. one-cent coin is struck in steel.

Thomas Jefferson Memorial in Washington D.C is Completed.

Great Depression ends in the United States: With unemployment figures falling fast due to World War II-related employment.

US General Dwight D. Eisenhower becomes the supreme Allied commander.

British deception plan " The Man Who Never Was" or Operation Mincement executed.

In the United States, it is announced that shoe rationing Canned food, meat, cheese, butter and cooking oils will go into effect.

1943 Calendar

January 1943
Sun	Mon	Tue	Wed	Thu	Fri	Sat
					1	2
3	4	5	6	7	8	9
10	11	12	13	14	15	16
17	18	19	20	21	22	23
24	25	26	27	28	29	30
31						

February 1943
Sun	Mon	Tue	Wed	Thu	Fri	Sat
	1	2	3	4	5	6
7	8	9	10	11	12	13
14	15	16	17	18	19	20
21	22	23	24	25	26	27
28						

March 1943
Sun	Mon	Tue	Wed	Thu	Fri	Sat
	1	2	3	4	5	6
7	8	9	10	11	12	13
14	15	16	17	18	19	20
21	22	23	24	25	26	27
28	29	30	31			

April 1943
Sun	Mon	Tue	Wed	Thu	Fri	Sat
				1	2	3
4	5	6	7	8	9	10
11	12	13	14	15	16	17
18	19	20	21	22	23	24
25	26	27	28	29	30	

May 1943
Sun	Mon	Tue	Wed	Thu	Fri	Sat
						1
2	3	4	5	6	7	8
9	10	11	12	13	14	15
16	17	18	19	20	21	22
23	24	25	26	27	28	29
30	31					

June 1943
Sun	Mon	Tue	Wed	Thu	Fri	Sat
		1	2	3	4	5
6	7	8	9	10	11	12
13	14	15	16	17	18	19
20	21	22	23	24	25	26
27	28	29	30			

July 1943
Sun	Mon	Tue	Wed	Thu	Fri	Sat
				1	2	3
4	5	6	7	8	9	10
11	12	13	14	15	16	17
18	19	20	21	22	23	24
25	26	27	28	29	30	31

August 1943
Sun	Mon	Tue	Wed	Thu	Fri	Sat
1	2	3	4	5	6	7
8	9	10	11	12	13	14
15	16	17	18	19	20	21
22	23	24	25	26	27	28
29	30	31				

September 1943
Sun	Mon	Tue	Wed	Thu	Fri	Sat
			1	2	3	4
5	6	7	8	9	10	11
12	13	14	15	16	17	18
19	20	21	22	23	24	25
26	27	28	29	30		

October 1943
Sun	Mon	Tue	Wed	Thu	Fri	Sat
					1	2
3	4	5	6	7	8	9
10	11	12	13	14	15	16
17	18	19	20	21	22	23
24	25	26	27	28	29	30
31						

November 1943
Sun	Mon	Tue	Wed	Thu	Fri	Sat
	1	2	3	4	5	6
7	8	9	10	11	12	13
14	15	16	17	18	19	20
21	22	23	24	25	26	27
28	29	30				

December 1943
Sun	Mon	Tue	Wed	Thu	Fri	Sat
			1	2	3	4
5	6	7	8	9	10	11
12	13	14	15	16	17	18
19	20	21	22	23	24	25
26	27	28	29	30	31